To Kaiden & Nora
With Love
G. G.

Itsy Bitsy & Teeny Weeny

Written by Robbyn Smith van Frankenhuyzen

Illustrated by Gijsbert van Frankenhuyzen

A Note from Robbyn

In 1980 we bought Hazel Ridge Farm. The following year we began rescuing injured and orphaned wildlife. It was a labor of love that not only spawned the Hazel Ridge series through the journals we kept, but also led us to change our 40-acre farm into a nature conservancy. Corn and oat fields became woodlots and open prairies. Pastures and soybean fields became ponds and wetlands. All that digging and planting meant safe habitat to release those rescued animals back into the wild.

Twenty-five years later, when our lives got busy with books and travel, we stopped animal rescue. It was one thing to ask someone to look after dogs, cats, horses, and sheep if we needed to travel out of the area but it was a bit much to expect someone to feed hawks, owls, fawns, opossums, skunks, coyotes, squirrels, rabbits, etc.

After *Adopted by an Owl* came out, *Saving Samantha* was next. Nick needed additional reference material for his paintings. That is when we found Louise Sagaert. She is owner, manager, and chief bottle washer of the Wildside Rehabilitation Center in Eaton Rapids, Michigan. Her dedication to helpless and injured animals is incredible. She has been in the business for

Louise at work.

years, though I use the word "business" lightly. She never charges anyone who drops off an animal. Funding for the center comes out of her own pocket and from donations. Over a six-month period she goes through hundreds of gallons of goat's milk (at $5.00 a gallon), thousands of mealworms, minnows, and mice to feed her wards.

Louise has a wonderful staff of volunteers; some have been with her for years. Like her, they all have that deep-in-their-gut desire to help helpless and injured animals. For more information about her work or to make a donation to the center, please direct questions to Wildside Rehabilitation and Education Center, 8601 Houston Road, Eaton Rapids, MI 48827.

The screen door banged loudly behind me, alerting the farm animals that morning chores were about to begin.

The sheep baah-ed loudly for their grain, the horse kicked up her heels, her tail a'flyin,' and the hens and chicks clucked and peeped. The barn cats, normally too busy with their own affairs, now circled my legs like I was their best friend.

It was business as usual at Hazel Ridge Farm. Yet in all the sameness, I knew there were always surprises to be had, especially in the spring.

I was eager to get to the barn. It was May and lambing time was nearly over. For weeks now black, woolly lambs were racing and bouncing with pure delight in the pasture. But one ewe, Woolly Mama, had yet to lamb.

Now, looking into her pen, I could see her time would be soon. The old ewe was restless. It seemed she would just settle down to rest, then she would get up again, circling and pawing. She was anxious for her lambs to be born. Her baah even sounded different. It was tender and soft as if she were already speaking to her babies.

"Well, old girl, it looks like your time will be comin' soon. You'll do just fine, Mama. I'll just leave you be and check in on you after chores."

After lunch I sneaked back into the barn and discovered Woolly Mama was the proud mother of twins. The lambs stood knock-kneed and wobbling as they nursed, Woolly Mama nuzzling their behinds.

"Nice job, Mama. A boy and a girl, eh? You have a beautiful family."
I offered her fresh hay and special grain, then tiptoed away.

The best thing I could do for her now was to give her some
peace and quiet to bond with her lambs.

Just about suppertime I went out for one last peek at the new family. Woolly Mama and her twins were lying peacefully in the far corner of her pen.

As I turned to leave, I spotted a tiny black lump in the darkest corner. I climbed into the pen for a closer look. A near-lifeless lamb lay there, apart from the family.

"A triplet," I whispered, picking up the limp body.

Cautiously, I walked over to Woolly Mama. "Here, Mama, she's yours. Sniff her."

Woolly Mama sniffed and snorted as if to say, *This doesn't belong to me*, and turned away.

"Come on now, girl," I offered again.

This time the ewe snorted, knocking the lamb away. I had seen this before. If a ewe doesn't bond right away with the lamb, it usually never does. This runt was too weak to compete with her stronger siblings. All of Woolly Mama's attention went to the healthy two.

This rejected runt was not going to be safe with her mother.

"Well, it looks like I'm your mama now."

I wrapped the tiny body in an old towel and nuzzled her nose. "You're such a teeny-weeny little girl. I've got a safe place for you in the house."

As licensed wildlife rehabilitators our house was like a hospital, with cages and equipment ready for any emergency. There was a playpen already set up, having been the recent home to a young fox kit that had been hit by a car. Sadly, it hadn't survived.

Now, as I made my way to the house, a rusty old truck clunked and rattled in the driveway. It sputtered to a stop.

A grizzled old man stuck his head out the window and asked, "You the folks that take care of wild critters?"

I cradled the lamb in my arms and said, "We are."

He lifted a speckled fawn from the front seat. "Nearly ran over this little feller in the hayfield. It's prit' near dead. Can you do somethin'?"

Mother Nature has a special way of caring for fawns. Their spots camouflage them in the tall grasses, and for their first three weeks of life they have no scent to them at all, keeping them safe from most predators. But there's not much that nature can do about tractors or well-meaning farmers.

I shifted the lamb in my arms to make room for the fawn. "Well, I suppose it will be just as easy to take care of two as it is one."

I said goodbye to the farmer and headed for the house.

I gently tucked the "twins" in the playpen lined with towels and plugged in the heating pad.

"You are brother and sister now. What shall we name you?"

I looked down at the tiny orphans curled together in a black-and-brown spotted ball.

"You, little lamb, will be Teeny Weeny and your brother will be Itsy Bitsy. There's not much life left in either one of you but let's give it our best shot, shall we?"

The first week was a struggle for the orphans. I slept on the couch next to their playpen, feeding them every hour.

At first they barely had enough energy to nurse from the bottle. The fresh goat's milk was rich with fat and nutrients but they only drank small amounts at each feeding. I often held them in my lap, hoping my touch would spark their will to live.

They grew stronger with each passing day. Their baahs and bleats became louder and more determined until finally, on the fifth day, they both stood on shaky legs to nurse.

After two weeks they had gained much strength and I was pleased with their improvement. "Good morning, little ones." The twins lifted their heads and scrambled to their feet.

"Well, look at you two. You're not so puny anymore, are you? It won't be long before you'll need to move to a bigger pen."

I scooped them out of their pen and set them on the floor. "Come on then, let's get breakfast."

Their pointy hooves skated over the slippery wooden floors as they followed me into the kitchen. A trail of round, brown "droppings" marked their path.

After three weeks I woke up one morning to a comical surprise. The twins had escaped from their playpen and were bouncing around the living room.

"Well, it looks like you two are ready for the barn."

Teeny Weeny and Itsy Bitsy pranced behind
me into the bright outdoors. I felt like Mary
from the nursery rhyme. Everywhere that
I went, the twins were "sure to go."

A large lambing pen in the barn was perfect.
And now the dogs, Buddy and Myles,
were eager to take on mothering
roles, too. They happily assumed
the job of cleaning their faces
after each meal.

Life was all about eating, sleeping, and playing for the twins. As the twins began eating more hay, they needed fewer bottle feedings until finally they were down to one bottle at breakfast and one at dinnertime.

After three weeks in their special pen, the twins were ready to join the rest of the flock. I led them down to the meadow to start the introductions.

The mothers snorted at the "intruders" and walked away, but the spring lambs leaped with joy at discovering new playmates.

It was all way too much for Teeny Weeny and Itsy Bitsy. They hid behind my legs for protection. But soon enough their curiosity won over their fear, and a lively game of tag began.

One morning as I started out on my usual walk with
the dogs, Teeny Weeny and Itsy Bitsy followed me
along the fence line.

"Look at you two. You're three months
old and ready to explore the world. Do
you want to join us?" I swung the
gate open and out they came.

And so I had company each day
on my morning walks. We made for
quite an unusual flock: a fawn, a lamb,
two dogs, a human, and sometimes a cat or
two. Our walks became quite an adventure.
Discovering frogs at the pond or snakes in
the grass got everyone leaping.

As summer passed, Teeny Weeny's black wool began to fade. Itsy Bitsy's spots were fading, too, and his coat was now a rich, golden brown.

I watched them butting heads in the pasture. While this playful ramming may have been a favorite game, later on it would mean serious business when Teeny Weeny became a protective mother and when Itsy Bitsy needed to defend his territory.

Wild deer started to notice Itsy Bitsy in the
pasture and jumped the fence to check him out.
The twins enjoyed their new company but the
rest of the flock kept a wary distance.

Then trouble started when Itsy Bitsy grew tall enough to jump the fence. He left poor Teeny Weeny baahing miserably on the other side. She didn't want to leave the safe pasture but she missed being with her brother.

Itsy Bitsy trampled through my vegetable garden, nibbling sunflowers and carrot tops.

He wasn't bad on purpose. He just didn't know any better.

I spent much of the summer shooing Itsy Bitsy back into the pasture. It was plain to see that the wildness in his nature tugged at him. He loved to explore beyond his boundaries.

By late fall the twins were nearly full-grown and it was getting harder to keep Itsy Bitsy out of trouble.

Angry neighbors complained about "that deer" eating their prize roses. He crossed roads with no concern for traffic, and when the neighborhood dogs chased him back to the pasture, he thought they were playing tag.

More and more I would find the young deer wandering outside the pasture and Teeny Weeny content to stay within the safety of the flock.

With hunting season approaching, I decide to block off a special area with a taller fence just for the two of them.

"I know it's less room than you're used to but it will have to do. You will be safer here. You two can keep each other company until hunting season is over. Then Itsy Bitsy, we'll work on getting you back in the wild where you belong."

The pen seemed to be escape-proof and I stopped worrying for the young deer's safety.

Winter wasn't too far off and all the farm animals began growing their warm winter coats. Itsy Bitsy had grown into a handsome young buck. But there was a restlessness in his eyes as he pranced along the fence line.

One snowy morning as I began my chores I heard Teeny Weeny's distressed baahing. I wondered what sort of trouble Itsy Bitsy had gotten himself into this time. When I reached the pen, I froze.

Itsy Bitsy had tried, unsuccessfully, to jump the fence and one leg had gotten caught in the wire. Now he was struggling to get free. I saw panic in his eyes and knew that if he didn't escape soon the leg would be broken.

There was no calming him down. I raced to the barn, grabbing a pair of wire cutters to cut the fence and release his leg.

By the time it was all over both Itsy Bitsy and I were covered with cuts and bruises. I dropped to the ground to catch my breath. He stood panting, lifting his injured leg.

"I'm so sorry," I whispered. "You are wild. You don't belong in a cage."

I sat there crying, tears stinging my face. I felt I had failed Itsy Bitsy miserably.

Right then and there I decided it was time to let him go free.

Hunting season was over. Mother Nature is a good provider. Itsy Bitsy was strong and clever: all that he needed to survive—food, shelter, and water—was all around us.

I knew he would be safe.

I pulled myself up and unlatched the gate.

After such a frightening experience, Itsy Bitsy wanted to stay clear of fences. But his instinct to leave was stronger than his fear.

He leaped through the open gate.

Teeny Weeny and I watched together in silence as Itsy Bitsy raced through the pasture and over the fence into the trees. The sheep's nose went up in the air and she let out a long, forlorn baah.

"I'll miss him, too, Teeny Weeny, but this is the way it is supposed to be. We did our part, now it's up to Itsy Bitsy. Wild animals are meant to be free."

Later that winter, I saw Itsy Bitsy one last time.
He had joined a herd of young bucks and, despite
his limp, looked healthy and strong.

I wanted to call out to him, but I knew it would be wrong. The deer was exactly where he was supposed to be...back in the wild.

For Noorah Cole,

May you always experience the joy, love, and magic of Hazel Ridge Farm.

Text Copyright © 2009 Robbyn Smith van Frankenhuyzen
Illustration Copyright © 2009 Gijsbert van Frankenhuyzen

Sleeping Bear Press™

315 East Eisenhower Parkway, Suite 200
Ann Arbor, MI 48108
www.sleepingbearpress.com

2009 © Sleeping Bear Press is an imprint of Gale, a part of Cengage Learning.

10 9 8 7 6 5 4 3

Library of Congress Cataloging-in-Publication Data

Frankenhuyzen, Robbyn Smith van.
Itsy Bitsy & Teeny Weeny / written by Robbyn Smith van Frankenhuyzen ;
illustrated by Gijsbert van Frankenhuyzen.
p. cm.
Summary: "A nature and animal rescue story that finds a lamb, rejected by its mother, and an
orphaned fawn being cared for by a farm family as siblings on Hazel Ridge Farm. Eventually the
animals separate, one back into the wild and the other a domestic animal"—Provided by publisher.
ISBN 978-1-58536-417-6
1. Lambs—Michigan—Anecdotes. 2. Fawns—Michigan—Anecdotes.
3. Animal rescue—Michigan—Anecdotes. I. Frankenhuyzen, Gijsbert van, ill. II. Title.
SF376.5.F73 2009
636.08'32--dc22   2008037826

Printed by China Translation & Printing Services Limited, Guangdong Province, China. 3rd printing.   07/2011